Governing the United States

Ask the Attorney General

Christy Mihaly

Rourke
Educational Media
rourkeeducationalmedia.com

A Division of
Carson Dellosa Education

ROURKE'S
SCHOOL to HOME
CONNECTIONS
BEFORE AND DURING READING ACTIVITIES

Before Reading: *Building Background Knowledge and Vocabulary*

Building background knowledge can help children process new information and build upon what they already know. Before reading a book, it is important to tap into what children already know about the topic. This will help them develop their vocabulary and increase their reading comprehension.

Questions and Activities to Build Background Knowledge:

1. Look at the front cover of the book and read the title. What do you think this book will be about?
2. What do you already know about this topic?
3. Take a book walk and skim the pages. Look at the table of contents, photographs, captions, and bold words. Did these text features give you any information or predictions about what you will read in this book?

Vocabulary: *Vocabulary Is Key to Reading Comprehension*

Use the following directions to prompt a conversation about each word.

- Read the vocabulary words.
- What comes to mind when you see each word?
- What do you think each word means?

Vocabulary Words:
- advise
- enforce
- federal
- immigration
- investigates
- lawyer
- legislatures
- rights

During Reading: *Reading for Meaning and Understanding*

To achieve deep comprehension of a book, children are encouraged to use close reading strategies. During reading, it is important to have children stop and make connections. These connections result in deeper analysis and understanding of a book.

 Close Reading a Text

During reading, have children stop and talk about the following:

- Any confusing parts
- Any unknown words
- Text to text, text to self, text to world connections
- The main idea in each chapter or heading

Encourage children to use context clues to determine the meaning of any unknown words. These strategies will help children learn to analyze the text more thoroughly as they read.

When you are finished reading this book, turn to the next-to-last page for **Text-Dependent Questions** and an **Extension Activity**.

TABLE OF CONTENTS

What Is the Attorney General's Job?

An attorney general (AG) is a **lawyer** who works in government. What is their job like? Ask the attorney general!

What does an attorney general do?

There is one attorney general for the United States government. The U.S. Attorney General is the top lawyer in the country. They uphold **federal** laws. There is also an attorney general for each U.S. state. These AGs **enforce** state laws.

OFFICE of the ATTORNEY GENERAL

What does the U.S. Attorney General do?

The U.S. AG has a big job. They are picked by the president to work in the executive branch of government. This branch is in charge of making sure that the laws of the United States are obeyed.

U.S. AGs

The United States has had more AGs than presidents. William Barr became the 85th U.S. AG in 2019. He was appointed by Donald Trump, the 45th president.

The U.S. AG runs the Department of Justice (DOJ). The DOJ **investigates** to find facts. It fights crime.

DOJ lawyers go to court. They represent the government. They make sure that the law is followed and that justice is done.

What does a state attorney general do?

State AGs are in state government. AGs study state problems. They **advise** the governor and other state leaders. They represent their state.

Some call the AG "the people's lawyer." AGs enforce laws that keep people safe and that protect the state's land and water. They help stop crime. AGs protect people's **rights**.

Letitia James, New York's state attorney general, talks to the public about a court ruling.

Attorneys General

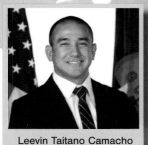

Leevin Taitano Camacho
Guam

Clare E. Connors
Hawaii

Leslie Rutledge
Arkansas

Karl A. Racine
Washington, D.C.

Denise N. George
U.S. Virgin Islands

Kwame Raoul
Illinois

These are just some of the AGs! Is one of them your AG?

What does an attorney general do at work?

AGs give advice about laws and talk with people on their teams. They go to meetings and read reports about what is happening in their communities. They explain their work and announce decisions.

The U.S. AG sometimes talks to Congress. State AGs talk to their **legislatures**. AGs know the law well. They discuss and give information about laws.

Laws are important in the United States. AGs help enforce those laws on a federal and state level. They support police officers and other law enforcement officials.

Who works for an attorney general?

Many people work on the AG's team. It includes lawyers, crime investigators, and office workers. Some people in the AG's office talk with news reporters and give information to the public.

Why Does the Attorney General Matter?

How can attorneys general help people?

AGs work on important issues. They fight hate crimes, work on gun laws, and stop polluters. AGs review and study laws. They suggest new laws or new ways to enforce the laws we have.

U.S. Attorney General Robert Kennedy speaks in support of equal rights for people of all races.

Do state attorneys general work together?

AGs work together to get things done. Together, AGs can stop sales of dangerous toys. They can work for cleaner air. They can improve **immigration** laws. State AGs have a stronger voice together.

The attorneys general of New York, Iowa, Washington, and Pennsylvania work together and speak to the press about a big settlement with tobacco companies.

In the 1990s, state AGs went to court and fought cigarette companies together. They said the companies broke laws. People in the U.S. were getting very sick from smoking cigarettes. AGs fought for cigarette companies to pay for doctor bills. They said that the sickness was the companies' fault. Eventually, the companies agreed to pay the states billions of dollars.

Interesting Things About Being Attorney General

What are the rules about being an AG?

Some states say the AG must be at least 30 years old. Other states say at least 18. Some states don't have any rule about age.

AG Firsts

Edmund Randolph was the first U.S. AG. George Washington appointed him in 1789.

Janet Reno was the first woman U.S. AG. She worked for President Bill Clinton. He appointed her in 1993.

Edmund Randolph

Janet Reno

In most states, voters elect AGs. In five states, the governor picks the AG. State AGs serve a four-year term, except in Vermont, where they serve for two years.

Kansas AG Derek Schmidt takes the oath of office for a third term in 2019.

Laws are important in the United States. AGs help enforce those laws. They make sure that government works for the people—including you!

Government of the United States

Attorneys general work in the executive branch. But they can advise the legislative branch too. Look at the chart and find people AGs can work with.

	Legislative Branch Makes the laws.	Executive Branch Carries out the laws.	Judicial Branch Decides what laws mean.
Federal Governs the whole country.	**Congress** Includes Senators and members of the House of Representatives.	**The President** Works with cabinet members such as the U.S. Attorney General.	**U.S. Courts** Judges work at many courts, including the U.S. Supreme Court.
State Governs each of the 50 states.	**State Legislature** Representatives work at the capitol building in each state's capital city.	**The Governor** Works with many officials such as the Secretary of State and the State Attorney General.	**State Courts** Include the highest court in the state—the state Supreme Court.
Local Governs each village, town, or city.	**City Council** Representatives make rules about how land is used, where roads will be built, and more.	**The City Mayor** Is in charge of the police department, the parks department, and more.	**Local Courts** Judges rule on cases that involve city laws and crimes that are less serious.

Glossary

advise (uhd-VIZE): to give someone information and suggestions

enforce (en-FORS): to make sure a law is obeyed

federal (FED-uh-ruhl): related to the government of an entire country, such as the government of the United States

immigration (im-i-GRAY-shuhn): the action of moving to another country permanently

investigates (in-VES-ti-gates): gathers information about someone or something that happened

lawyer (LAW-yur or LOI-ur): a person who has studied the law and is trained to advise people about the law and represent people in court

legislatures (LEJ-is-lay-churs): groups of people who make or change laws for a country or state

rights (rites): claims or actions that a person deserves or is entitled to, such as the right to vote, the right to equal treatment, or the right to free speech

Index

Text-Dependent Questions

1. Name three tasks of the U.S. Attorney General.

2. Name three things a state attorney general might do.

3. What are three differences between a state AG and the U.S. AG?

4. How can AGs work together?

5. Why is the AG's work important?

Extension Activity

The U.S. Attorney General's office has an online form for public comments: https://www.justice.gov/contact-us. Find out what issues the U.S. AG is working on. Check your state website to see how to contact your state AG. Learn what your state AG is working on. Then, write to the U.S. or state AG. Tell them what you think about issues they are working on.

ABOUT THE AUTHOR

Christy Mihaly worked as a lawyer for two different state attorneys general. In 2007 the National Association of Attorneys General awarded her the Laurie Loveland Award for her work. Now she's an author. She has written many nonfiction books for young readers, including *Free for You and Me*, a picture book about the First Amendment to the U.S. Constitution. Find out more or say hello at www.christymihaly.com.

PHOTO CREDITS: Cover: ©Ultima_Gaina; page 5: ©powerofforever; page 6: ©MathewTNichols; page 7: ©wingedwolf; page 8: ©lev radin; page 9a: ©Wiki; page 9b: ©Clare Conners; page 9c: ©Gage Skidmore; page 9d: ©KeaTaylor; page 9e: ©ErinKlee; page 10: ©Cecilie_Arcurs; page 11: ©Li Kim Gon; page 12: ©Susan Chiang; page 13: ©Steve Debenport; page 14: ©ericsphotography; page 15: ©Wiki; page 16: ©Pete Souza/Chicago Tribune; page 17: ©4x6; page 18a: ©Edmund Randolph; page 19: ©Mark Reinstein; page 20: ©Utah778

Edited by: Madison Capitano
Cover design by: Rhea Magaro-Wallace
Interior design by: Janine Fisher

Library of Congress PCN Data

Ask the Attorney General / Christy Mihaly (Governing the United States)
ISBN 978-1-73162-914-2 (hard cover)
ISBN 978-1-73162-913-5 (soft cover)
ISBN 978-1-73162-915-9 (e-Book)
ISBN 978-1-73163-350-7 (ePub)
Library of Congress Control Number: 2019944960

Rourke Educational Media
Printed in the United States of America,
North Mankato, Minnesota